GROWING UP

PROTECTED

Created and Produced by Firecrest Books Ltd
in association with John Francis/Bernard Thornton Artists

Copyright © 2001 Firecrest Books Ltd
and Copyright © 2001 John Francis/Bernard Thornton Artists

Published by Tangerine Press™, an imprint of Scholastic Inc.
555 Broadway, New York, NY 10012

Tangerine Press™ and associated logo and design are trademarks of Scholastic Inc.

ISBN 0-439-30531-4

Printed and bound in Belgium
First printing, September 2001

GROWING UP

PROTECTED

Bernard Stonehouse

Illustrated by
John Francis

TANGERINE PRESS™ and associated logo
and design are trademarks of Scholastic Inc.

FOR ROSS

Art and Editorial Direction by
Peter Sackett

Designed by
Paul Richards, Designers & Partners

Edited by
Norman Barrett

Color separation by
Sang Choy International Pte. Ltd.
Singapore

Printed and bound by
Casterman, Belgium

CONTENTS

Introduction

This tiger cub, just a few weeks old, looks out at a strange and none-too-friendly world. Before long it will be a big tiger, better able to cope with whatever comes its way. Right now it is just a little one, depending for its life on the protection of grown-ups, particularly on the care of its mother's instincts, skills, and strong paws. One of the rules of life is that practically all animals start out much smaller than their parents. The smaller they are, the more enemies there are to hurt, damage, or eat them. If they are to survive at all, young animals need protection, and different kinds of animals protect their young in different ways. This book shows some of the ways in which grown-up animals protect their young during the first few days, months, or years of life.

Parents offer protection and the young respond, using both the instincts they were born with and the tricks they learn as they go along. Right now this little tiger's instinct is to sit quietly between those big, protective paws and watch the world go by. That gives it a chance to learn. From parental protection and care, it will learn a great deal very quickly during the next few months.

Jewel fish

Some call them jewel fish because of their brilliant gem-like colors. At 3 to 4 inches (7.5 to 10 cm) long, they are popular as aquarium pets. Others call them "mouth-brooders," because of the curious way they have of protecting their young. The mother fish holds her mouth open, and the little fish swim in to safety.

They are not unique. Several other kinds of fish within the same family have developed the same trick. Jewel fish lay their eggs among stones on a clean rock or on sand, and both parents guard them. When the eggs hatch – several dozen of them – the little ones emerge and start hunting for tiny insects and other fragments of food close to the nest. If a shadow falls across them, or any other sign of danger threatens, they swim to the nearest brightly colored object, which is certain to be their mother. Where can she hide them? There is no handy cave or weed. So she opens her mouth, and they find safety inside. It works well when they are tiny. Sometimes when they are bigger, she forgets what it is all about – and swallows them. That is carrying protection a little too far.

Jewel fish lay their eggs in rows on the lake or stream bed, guarding them until they hatch.

The hatchlings never stray far from their mother.

8

Musk ox

These strange, cattlelike animals with crumpled horns, are distant kin of cows and sheep. Because of their musty smell, they are called musk oxen. They live in the Arctic, usually in the coldest, driest, and windiest parts they can find. It sounds uncomfortable, but it's where the snow lies thinnest on the ground. Musk oxen cannot dig down through thick, heavy snow to find food. They browse year-round on the thin tundra vegetation, feeding heavily in summer, but living on a near-starvation diet in winter.

Musk oxen form family herds of a dozen or so adults. The calves, born into this cold, windy world in early spring, browse alongside their parents and shelter between them from the wind. When hungry wolves prowl around the herds in the hope of a meal, the adults form a ring facing outward, with the calves in the middle. Crumpled or not, those horns are sharp and powerful, and a match for any wolf.

When adult musk oxen form a circle around their calves, the predatory wolves face a ring of horns and lowered heads.

Even newborn musk ox calves are well covered in dense woolly fur, to keep them warm on the cold Arctic tundra.

African lion

The African veldt, or open grassland, is a dangerous place for growing up, even if you are the son or daughter of the King of Beasts. Lions are top predators on the veldt, taking their pick of the smaller grass-eating antelopes, tackling even the young of the larger gnus, giraffes, and zebras. So who is brave enough to eat young lions?

Lionesses produce litters of two, three, or four cubs, usually in a den. This could be a hollow among rocks or a safe place under a bush, some distance from her "pride," or family group. The mother keeps in touch with her group, but returns to the cubs several times daily to wash and feed them. Soon after they are born, she picks up each cub gently in her mouth and carries them to another den. After two or three days, she moves them again, and again until they are able to walk at her heels. She is protecting them against hyenas, jackals, and perhaps even snakes, which hunt by scent and might find the cubs in a well-used, smelly den. She may even be protecting them against the male lion that rules her pride. A newcomer that has chased out an older male may seek and destroy small cubs, so that he can mate quickly with the mothers and start families of his own. For one reason or another, it is safest to keep moving.

It takes five to seven years for cubs to grow to maturity. Much of the time, they are learning within the protection of the pride.

For the first few weeks of their lives, the mother looks after her cubs and protects them from predators.

Mute swan

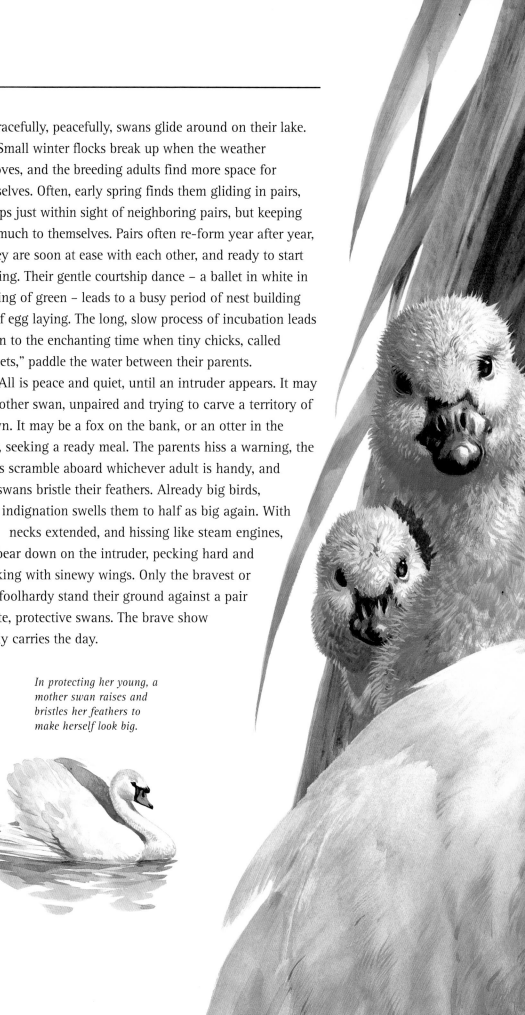

Gracefully, peacefully, swans glide around on their lake. Small winter flocks break up when the weather improves, and the breeding adults find more space for themselves. Often, early spring finds them gliding in pairs, perhaps just within sight of neighboring pairs, but keeping very much to themselves. Pairs often re-form year after year, so they are soon at ease with each other, and ready to start breeding. Their gentle courtship dance – a ballet in white in a setting of green – leads to a busy period of nest building and of egg laying. The long, slow process of incubation leads in turn to the enchanting time when tiny chicks, called "cygnets," paddle the water between their parents.

All is peace and quiet, until an intruder appears. It may be another swan, unpaired and trying to carve a territory of its own. It may be a fox on the bank, or an otter in the water, seeking a ready meal. The parents hiss a warning, the chicks scramble aboard whichever adult is handy, and both swans bristle their feathers. Already big birds, indignation swells them to half as big again. With necks extended, and hissing like steam engines, they bear down on the intruder, pecking hard and smacking with sinewy wings. Only the bravest or most foolhardy stand their ground against a pair of irate, protective swans. The brave show usually carries the day.

Newly hatched cygnets hitch rides aboard their parents, especially when danger threatens.

Cygnets grow quickly from fluffy chicks to near adult size in about 3 months.

In protecting her young, a mother swan raises and bristles her feathers to make herself look big.

14

Woolly opossum

We usually think of marsupials as large, kangaroo-like animals that leap around Australia. But marsupials come in all proportions, from mouse size upward, and several families of small, tree-living marsupials of squirrel to rabbit size are found in South America. Some of these extend north through Panama to Mexico and the United States. This woolly opossum is a small South American marsupial that runs and climbs trees. It is one of three closely related species that live in tropical forests from northern Brazil to Mexico.

Woolly opossums are mild, not-too-bright, little animals. They eat leaves and insects, and seldom go out of their way to pick quarrels. Like their distant cousins in Australia, they keep their five or six newborn young in a small pouch – their first way of protecting them against the dangers of the forest. When the young grow too big to fit in, they cling firmly to their mother as she forages along the branches. As they grow bigger still, only two or three can climb aboard. So the rest follow closely, clinging by their tails to the branches. Mild they may be, but the mother's long jaws are full of sharp teeth that, together with her sharp claws, are ready at a moment's notice to protect her brood.

Mother clings upside down among the foliage while her small babies cling to her stomach.

Her long jaws, full of pin-sharp teeth, are formidable weapons in the woolly opossum's defense.

African jacana

Jacanas are long-legged water birds, related to curlews and other waders. They forage in ponds, streams, and lakes of several tropical countries. We find them, for example, in South America, southern Africa, India, Indonesia, and Australia. Often strikingly colored, they seldom live far from water. If you see such a bird apparently striding on the surface of a pond, on long, slender toes, it is almost certainly a jacana. In fact, it is walking on the waterweeds, with the long toes spreading its weight so that it does not sink.

That is not the jacana's only peculiarity. Females are often larger than males and always dominant. While both parents build the nest, only the male incubates the three or four eggs. Indeed, the hen may leave the male in charge, forming a partnership with a second male and laying a second clutch of eggs. The flimsy, floating nest, built of loosely woven grass and reeds, is by no means waterproof. To keep the eggs dry, the male tucks them under his wings. On hatching, the chicks quickly leave the nest – not surprisingly, because it must be damp and uncomfortable – and forage in the care of the male. If danger threatens, he tucks his family under his wings and strides off across the pond to safety.

The jacana's eggs, laid on a floating nest, have a glossy shell to help keep the water out.

Jacana chicks have very long toes to spread their weight over waterweeds growing just below the surface.

Imperial scorpion

There are more than 600 different kinds of scorpions in the world, living mostly in dry, tropical countries. Many are small, less than 1 inch (2.5 cm) long when fully grown. The largest grow up to 8 inches (20 cm) long. Scorpions have eight legs, and are closely related to spiders. They possess a large pair of pincers, used for grasping and fighting. The flat, low-slung body just clears the ground when they walk. The long tail curves upward, carrying a stinger on the end like a lantern. It is the stinger that has earned scorpions their bad reputation. A sting is always very painful, and can even kill a person.

That would be an accident, for scorpions do not lie in wait for people. Their main business is to catch the insects and spiders on which they feed. But they often enter houses, and they like to hide in comfortable cavities like shoes and cupboards. When scorpions are around, always shake your slippers before you put them on. They hunt mainly at night, fiercely attacking beetles, bugs, and spiders and tearing them to pieces. Female scorpions may even tear their own mates to pieces. But they make tender, caring mothers. Their young, born alive, are carried safely on their mother's back for several days, until they are old enough to fend for themselves.

The stinger contains a poison that is normally used to paralyze insects or spiders.

Polar bear

Here is a family that lives by hunting and foraging in harsh, cold Arctic lands where food is seldom plentiful. Polar bears live by their wits. It takes many months for them to learn how and where to hunt, and years before they are competent to survive alone. So these young bears will need their mother's protection for a long time yet.

Polar bears are born in litters of two or three, usually in snow caves carved by the mother in autumn. She sleeps through the winter, waking only for a few minutes at the birth. The little bears, no bigger than rabbits, find her warm milk supply and draw on it sleepily for the next few weeks. After about three months, the family emerges from their cave into the cold Arctic spring. The young bears follow their mother in long rambling walks that take them over the tundra and out onto the sea ice. Lesson one is that, in the Arctic almost anything is good to eat. They learn to catch seals, dig for berries, and find anything else, from ducks' eggs to dead whales, that will keep hungry bears alive. One of this family has already died of hunger. It will be two years, possibly even three, before the two remaining cubs are able to go their separate ways.

Polar bears are born in a den in the side of a snowdrift, kept warm by their sleeping mother's body heat.

The young bears follow their mother closely, learning about survival from everything she does.

Bottle-nosed dolphin

They are called "bottle-nosed" because their long snout reminded sailors of a long-necked bottle. Bottle-nosed dolphins, which are sea mammals, grow up to 12 feet (nearly 4 m) long. They live in warm temperate seas, from the East Coast of the United States to West Africa, and throughout the Mediterranean Sea and northward to France and Great Britain. Like most other dolphins, bottle-nosed dolphins hunt in groups of a dozen or more. These sometimes congregate to form huge "mobs" of several hundred. We come closest to them in marine parks, where they are often kept as performing animals.

Being mammals, dolphins breathe air. They must come to the surface every few minutes to breathe through the blowhole on top of their head. Baby dolphins are born tail first. As soon as a pup emerges from its mother's birth canal, she must push it quickly with her nose to the sea surface, so it can take its first breath of air. Otherwise it will drown. Often other dolphins, squeaking and chattering among themselves, help to ensure the baby makes a good start to its life as a marine mammal.

Dolphins protect their young from sharks by swimming between them and bumping the predator hard with their nose.

When danger threatens, the young cluster together and the adults circle protectively around them.

24

Common earwig

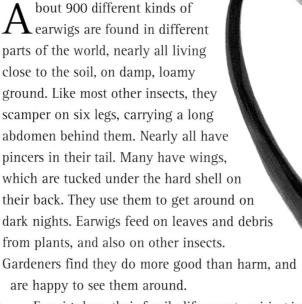

About 900 different kinds of earwigs are found in different parts of the world, nearly all living close to the soil, on damp, loamy ground. Like most other insects, they scamper on six legs, carrying a long abdomen behind them. Nearly all have pincers in their tail. Many have wings, which are tucked under the hard shell on their back. They use them to get around on dark nights. Earwigs feed on leaves and debris from plants, and also on other insects. Gardeners find they do more good than harm, and are happy to see them around.

Earwigs keep their family life secret, pairing in tiny chambers and cavities within the soil, where the females also lay their clutches of several dozen tiny eggs. Unusually for insects, earwig mothers take great care of their eggs, piling them together, cleaning and fussing over them, and defending them strongly against intruders. For the mother, this is a full-time task. Fathers have nothing to do with their young, and indeed are driven off if they try. The mother stays with her eggs for the month or more of incubation. They then hatch into nymphs, which look like short, stocky, underdeveloped earwigs. The mother fusses over them, too, until they molt, mature, and scamper off to fend for themselves. Then she can relax and feed, and perhaps start preparing for the next brood.

Females care for their eggs and nymphs in an underground nest, where they are well protected from weather and predators.

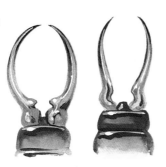

The nymphs shed their skin twice before leaving the nest, and several times more before becoming adults.

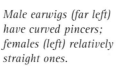

Male earwigs (far left) have curved pincers; females (left) relatively straight ones.

Giant anteater

Several different kinds of mammals specialize in eating ants and termites. There is not much nourishment in a single ant, but an ant nest may hold millions of them, plus eggs, grubs, and other food in store. To make a living from ant-eating, you first need to live where there are plenty of ant nests. You need to find the nests, break into them, and extract the ants in bulk. That is how giant anteaters live, and why they are such a strange shape.

Giant anteaters live in the northern half of South America, where there are plenty of ants and termites. Those long, pointed noses snuffle over the ground, finding the nests by scent. Then the big, curved claws come into action, to open up the nests by digging. The long tongue, coated with sticky saliva, sweeps around the nest like a long-handled broom, pulling ants into the narrow mouth. There are skills in all these actions, and skills have to be learned. Anteaters usually rear one baby at a time. The mother carries it on her back until it is a year old and well over half-grown. The young one watches carefully how its mother finds food. It starts to join in, and soon figures out how to catch ants for itself.

A young anteater watches as its mother flexes her claws to open an ant nest.

During the rainy season, giant anteaters swim flooded rivers to the safety of high ground.

Rabbit

Rabbits originated in Europe, but have spread with people all over the world. They multiply quickly – a pair can rear several hundred in a year. A lot of them together can destroy farm crops and pastures, and farmers sometimes have to kill them by the thousands. One reason for their success is the care and protection that mother rabbits give to their babies in the nest.

Rabbits live in groups of burrows called warrens. A small warren has just a few burrows, a big one may have several hundred. Each doe (female) has her own burrow, and each burrow has a nesting chamber. The doe lines this with grass and her own fur. She gives birth to between three and eight babies, and defends them fiercely against attacks by weasels, stoats, foxes, and other rabbits, which may try to steal the burrow. After about two weeks, the young rabbits surface for the first time. The doe stays with them until, at about five weeks, they become independent and go their own way. In 12 to 16 weeks they are ready to dig their own burrows and start breeding.

The nest is an underground cavern, in a burrow that the doe defends against predators.

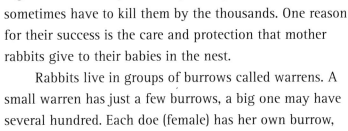

She feeds them on her milk until ...

... they are big enough to surface and start feeding themselves.

Raccoon

You see these little animals in many parts of the United States. About 30 inches (76 cm) long from their black nose to the tip of their stripy tail, they live in trees and open country. They feed on earthworms, insects, frogs, lizards, birds and their eggs, and a wide range of plants. Raccoons raid orchards, gardens, and cornfields when the crops are ripe, and they take well to town life, making themselves unpopular by raiding garbage cans. Their long, fingerlike claws enable them to hold small objects and examine them closely, perhaps intelligently, with their sharp, beady eyes.

You might think that the wider its range of food, the easier it would be for an animal to make a living. This may not be so. The wider the range, the more a young animal has to learn about different foods, how to hunt safely without exposing itself to predators, and how to avoid harmful food or poison. While young rabbits can be independent at 5 to 6 weeks (page 30), young raccoons at that age are still lying helpless in the den where they were born. They emerge for the first time at 10 to 12 weeks, and spend almost all of their first year with their mother, learning all the tricks of survival that a young raccoon needs to know.

Raccoons like to live close to water, where they can hunt for crayfish and insects.

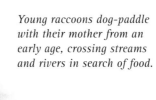

Young raccoons dog-paddle with their mother from an early age, crossing streams and rivers in search of food.

Japanese macaque

Macaques are monkeys of the Asian forests, from India to China, and from southern Indonesia to central Japan. Most are reddish-brown or black, with a head and body 18 to 24 inches (45 to 60 cm) long. Some have beards, others bare faces. Some have long tails, others short, stumpy tails. They use their tails for balancing as they leap and swing through the trees. Macaques live in troops of a dozen or more, foraging on leaves, plant shoots, insects, and a range of other foods from lizards to birds' eggs. Within each troop are several small family groups that keep together for mutual protection.

Japanese macaques are a separate species that live wild on the southern and central islands of Japan. Short-tailed, with expressive pink faces, they band together sometimes in huge troops of 100 or more, especially where food is plentiful. Males and females form pairs that seldom stay long together, but the infants are brought up within family groups.

Mothers feed and carry their own young. If danger threatens – a predatory hawk or owl, or a rival troop intent on stealing food – a horde of sisters, cousins, aunts, uncles, grandparents, and interested neighbors rally around. Shouting, screaming, and leaping up and down, they set up a hullabaloo that, often enough, drives the danger away.

Japanese macaque mothers carefully tend their own offspring, nursing and feeding them on milk.

Young macaques find plenty of friends of their own age within the troop.

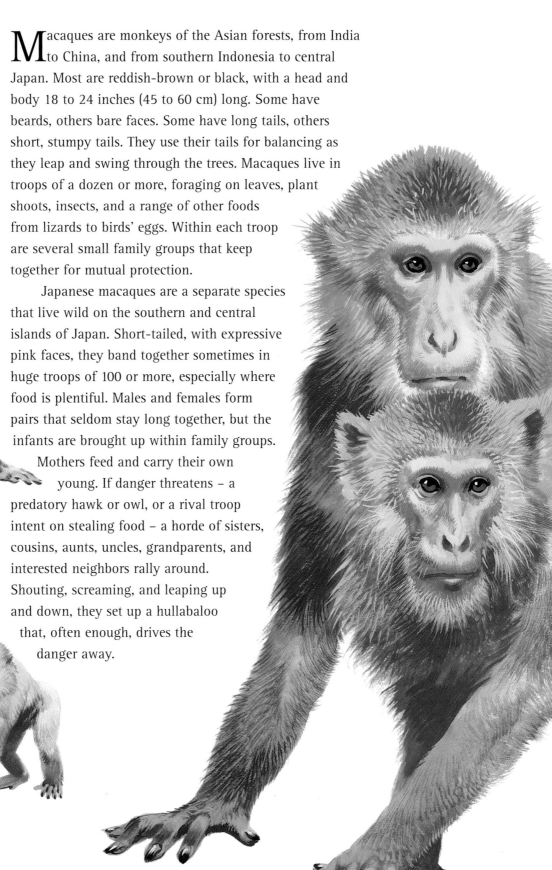

Gray wolf

Doglike animals with solid bodies and long legs, gray wolves live in the forests of northern Canada, Alaska, Yellowstone National Park, and Siberia. They usually move in loose packs of a dozen or more because a single wolf is vulnerable to predators, and cannot tackle large animals alone. A dozen together protect one another, and can bring down caribou or deer to provide a feast for all.

Young are born in litters of 4 to 10 cubs. After tending them for a month or so in a den, the mother brings them out to run with the pack. Now they must learn not only how to keep up, but also the rules that allow them to live together in harmony. Cubs play and fight together, learning how to tolerate and be tolerated by others. They find that tail-up means a cheerful "Hi" to their friends, but is a threat to their leader. It is better to approach him submissively, with tail down, ready to roll over to show you know he's the boss. An older wolf curling his lips is threatening, "Keep out of my way." You may be first at a kill, but stand back and let the leader feed first. It is like learning manners, and probably just as boring. But it saves trouble and makes life easier in the long run.

Litters are born in caves or dens away from the pack, tended by their mother for the first few weeks.

Emerging from the den, young cubs have to learn how to tolerate one another and live within the protection of the pack.

King cobra

A mother cobra curls up close to her eggs, ready to defend them from predators.

Newly hatched cobras are ready to hunt as soon as they leave the nest. This one has caught and is killing a smaller snake.

Cobras are venomous snakes, up to 7 feet 6 inches (2.3 m) long, with a distinctive "hood" – a flattened neck. When aroused by disturbance or the sight of prey, they rear their head and neck upright above the ground, ready to strike with poison-loaded fangs – their front teeth. Injected into flesh, the poison attacks the victim's nervous system and may kill within a few minutes. Cobras attack frogs, other snakes, lizards, birds, and small mammals for food. They defend themselves against disturbance from larger animals, including people.

Cobras pair with a mating dance that at first looks aggressive, but ends with the two lying side by side in harmony. The female finds a hole or cavity on the ground or perhaps in a tree trunk, where she lays 6 to 20 white, soft-shelled eggs. These she guards carefully – a female cobra that appears in the same place every day is almost certainly tending a nest, and is vulnerable to her greatest enemy, people. She will hiss a warning and strike at any animal that comes by. When the hatchlings, about 10 inches (25 cm) long, break out of the eggs, the mother's work is done. They have nothing to learn from her. Hunting and striking come naturally to them. They need only practice. Fueled by a small residue of yolk from the egg, within a few hours they will be foraging successfully for themselves.

Capybara

Imagine a gray-brown guinea pig as big as a large dog, with coarse fur and a superior, nose-in-the-air expression. That is a capybara. They are found in rain forests from Panama and Mexico to Brazil. Big ones stand up to 20 inches (50 cm) tall at the shoulder, and weigh over 110 pounds (50 kg).

Gentle animals that graze along riverbanks and lake edges, capybaras feed on grass and water plants, talking quietly to each other in grunts and squeaks. When alarmed, they give shrill warning barks, dive into the water and disappear. Well, nearly disappear – their trick is to swim almost completely submerged. Only the ears, eyes, and nostrils, all lined up along the top of the head, appear at the surface. With everything else out of sight, they can still listen, watch, and breathe.

Female capybaras produce litters of four to eight piglets, all very well developed. Within a few hours, they can swim alongside their parents. When several females produce litters at the same time, the piglets run together in a commune. All the mothers care equally for them, and all keep alert to give warning of danger.

Young capybaras may take milk not just from their own mother, but from other mothers in the group.

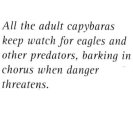

All the adult capybaras keep watch for eagles and other predators, barking in chorus when danger threatens.

Koala

Here is everyone's favorite cuddly animal. It looks like a live teddy bear. And because it eats eucalyptus leaves, it has a comfortable cough-drop scent. It is a koala. Some people call them koala bears, though they are not at all closely related to real bears.

Koalas live in the forests of northeastern Australia, where they spend nearly all their time clinging to the trunks and branches of eucalyptus trees, feeding on the leaves and shoots. Like kangaroos, wombats, opossums, and most other native mammals of Australia, they are marsupials. This means they give birth to very tiny babies – usually one at a time – so small that they are not even fully formed, and keep them for weeks in a furry pouch. Koala babies are less than 1 inch (2.5 cm) long at birth, and weigh only a fraction of an ounce – just big and strong enough to crawl into the pouch, which opens downward. At first, the baby koala is permanently attached to the milk gland, so it can feed whenever it is hungry. After two or three months, it is big enough to pop in and out of the pouch, and take an interest in the rest of the world. This one, about six months old, is still closely protected, holding tightly to its mother with clawed fingers and toes.

This young koala has entered the backward-facing pouch for a rest and a feed of milk.

At five or six months, a cub can be left to sleep safely by itself in the fork of a tree.

African elephant

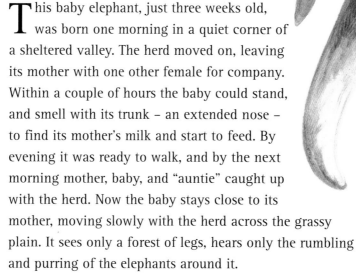

This baby elephant, just three weeks old, was born one morning in a quiet corner of a sheltered valley. The herd moved on, leaving its mother with one other female for company. Within a couple of hours the baby could stand, and smell with its trunk – an extended nose – to find its mother's milk and start to feed. By evening it was ready to walk, and by the next morning mother, baby, and "auntie" caught up with the herd. Now the baby stays close to its mother, moving slowly with the herd across the grassy plain. It sees only a forest of legs, hears only the rumbling and purring of the elephants around it.

For the moment, life is serious. Since birth, the baby has put on several pounds, and its legs are quite a bit longer and stronger. But it has a hard task staying with the herd, keeping out of the way of those moving feet and whisking tails. From time to time, it reaches up for a warm feed. In a few days' time it will become more adventurous – dawdling as the herd moves on, rolling and playing in the mud, and drinking, swimming, and showering in the river at dusk.

A mother elephant helps her newborn baby to its feet. The baby weighs about 200 lbs. (91 kg), and stands 3 ft. (1 m) tall.

Joining the herd, the baby hangs on to its mother's tail.

Young elephants take time off to play together in the mud.

American beaver

These American beavers live in the forests of northern North America. A similar species is found in Scandinavia and western Siberia. Beavers live near rivers and streams, in "lodges" that they build as homes from thin tree trunks and branches. They gnaw and fell the trees with their front teeth, tugging them into position and packing mud between to make them watertight. The lodges, containing passages and dry sleeping chambers, are constantly maintained by adding more branches. They form dams, which raise the level of the river and cause local flooding. The beavers feed on vegetation that grows on the flood plains.

Young beavers stay with their parents for two years at least, living in the lodge and taking part in the constant maintenance work. Like nest-building birds, beavers need no special training. A few inborn behavior patterns, such as gnawing trees close to the water, help them produce a serviceable lodge. It is doubtful that the adults set out to teach their young how to build.

But working in harmony with easygoing, tolerant parents, the young will learn what busy beavers do all day to make a safe, comfortable, and lasting home. Then they'll go and do it for themselves.

Beavers are protective parents – this one is carrying her cub to keep it dry.

Mother and cubs swim together in the water, diving to reach the dry chamber inside their lodge.

Index